HOW TO MAKE A STORY

Naomi Jones   ana Gómez

OXFORD
UNIVERSITY PRESS

Milo wanted a story.

Mum said he could choose a book from the shelf.
But Milo wanted a brand new story, just for him.

'Why don't you make one up?'
suggested Mum.

But Milo didn't know how.
And he was worried about getting it wrong.

'You can't get stories wrong,' Mum told him.
'You just need a beginning, a middle, and an end.'

'Can you help me with the beginning?' he asked.

Mum had a little think.

"It could be about a boy called . . .'

'WOLF!' shouted Milo.

Then he raced out into the
garden to look for ideas.

'I'm making up an amazing story
about a boy called Wolf,' Milo told Nana.

'What happens next?' she asked.
'Um . . . I don't know,' said Milo.

'People in stories often want something,' said Nana.

Milo thought and thought,
and then he had an idea—Wolf wanted
to find lots of shiny treasure!

TREASURE!

It was BIG and gold AND very shiny but there was a super-scary tiger guarding it!

Luckily, Wolf was really brave,
so he crawled forwards.
The tiger's tail twitched and then she . . .

Milo ran inside.
'I'm making up a story,' he told Dad.
'It's AWESOME, but I don't know
what happens in the middle.'

'Well,' said Dad, 'the middle is usually
where things get trickier and more exciting.'

Milo looked around for his next idea . . .

It didn't take him
long to find one.

CRASH! RUMBLE! BANG!

Just then, another idea popped into Milo's head.

Wolf started climbing a really, really, REALLY **big** mountain.

But . . .

Milo thought his story was amazing, but he wasn't sure how to end it. So, he went upstairs to look for ideas.

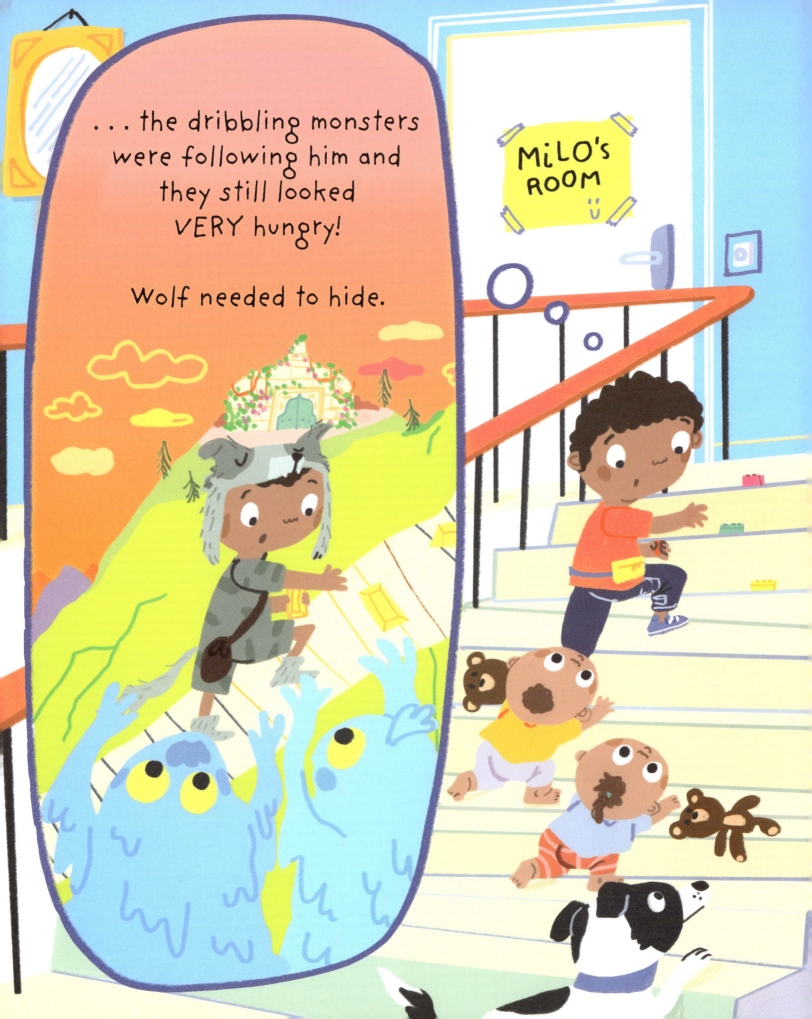

... the dribbling monsters were following him and they still looked VERY hungry!

Wolf needed to hide.

MiLO's ROOM

Milo hid in his den and looked
at all the bricks he'd collected.
Then he thought about Wolf's treasure.

Maybe Wolf could make something with the treasure,
just like how you make a story from words.

Perhaps it would help him find his ending?

So, Milo put all his bricks
into a pile and began to build.

Wolf made a gold chest
from the treasure . . .

...But while he was busy,
the dribbling monsters found him!

Wolf realised they didn't actually look hungry, they looked sad.

So he decided to share his treasure with them to cheer them up!

Finally, there was just one thing for Milo to say . . .

'The End!'

It had been lots of fun
making up his own story from
beginning to **middle** to **end.**

And now Milo had another idea . . .

FREYA

... after all, stories are so much better when they're shared!

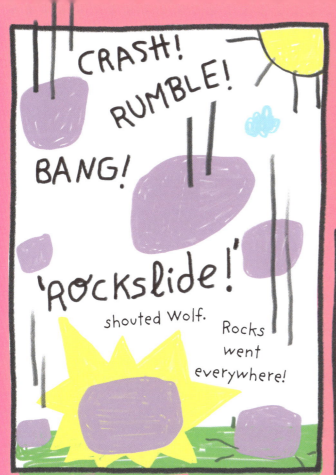

CRASH!
RUMBLE!
BANG!

'Rockslide!'

shouted Wolf.

Rocks went everywhere!

Under the rocks he spotted more shiny treasure. But . . .

. . . there were two slimy, dribbling MONSTERS behind Wolf and they wanted to eat him up!

'HELP!'
yelled Wolf.

How was he going to escape?

'Ah ha!'
'Look! Bears!'
Wolf said.

While the monsters were busy with the bears, he ran away.

Wolf started climbing a really, really, REALLY big mountain. But the dribbling monsters were following him and they still looked VERY hungry! Wolf needed to hide.

Wolf made a gold chest from the treasure.

But while he was busy, the dribbling monsters found him!

Wolf realised they didn't actually look hungry, they looked sad.

So he decided to share his treasure with them to cheer them up!

The End

After sharing his story with his
brother and sister, Milo knew just where
to keep it safe until it was story time again.

The End

OXFORD
UNIVERSITY PRESS

Oxford is a registered trademark
of Oxford University Press in the UK
and certain other countries

Words © Naomi Jones, 2023
Illustrations © Ana Gomez, 2023

British Library Cataloguing
in Publication Data

Data available

ISBN: 978-0-19-277904-5

Printed in China

www.oup.com

FOR MUM AND DAD, WHO HELPED ME
FALL IN LOVE WITH STORIES — NAOMI JONES

FOR MY STORY LOVER, SERGIO — GOMEZ